National Curriculum

Key Stage 1
Age 6–7 years

Prepare Your Child for

Key Stage 1 National Tests
ENGLISH: READING

1998 edition

Every effort has been made to trace copyright holders and to obtain their permission for the use of copyright material. The author and publishers will gladly receive any information enabling them to rectify any error or omission in subsequent editions.

First published 1997
Reprinted 1997
Revised 1997

Letts Educational
Aldine House
Aldine Place
London W12 8AW
Telephone: 0181-740 2266
e-mail: mail@lettsed.co.uk
website: http://www.lettsed.co.uk

Text: © BPP (Letts Educational) Ltd 1997
Author: Sarah Harris
The publishers gratefully acknowledge Judith Morris, Sally Murby and Wendy Bloom for their contributions.

Prepared by *specialist* publishing services, Milton Keynes

Design and illustrations:
© BPP (Letts Educational) Ltd 1997
Page layout: Tim Lole
Illustrations: Tim Lole
Original page design by
Ian Foulis Associates, Saltash

All our Rights Reserved. No part of this publication may be reproduced, stored in a retrieval system, or transmitted, in any form or by any means, electronic, mechanical, photocopying, recording or otherwise, without the prior permission of Letts Educational.

Acknowledgements
Frogs' Holiday written and illustrated by Margaret Gordon, published by Puffin Viking 1986, reprinted with permission; *Mrs Wobble the Waitress*, written by Allan Ahlberg and illustrated by Janet Ahlberg, published by Puffin Viking 1988, reprinted with permission.

British Library Cataloguing in Publication Data
A CIP record for this book is available from the British Library.
ISBN 1 85758 745 6
Printed in Great Britain by Livesey Ltd, Shrewsbury
Letts Educational is the trading name of
BPP (Letts Educational) Ltd

CONTENTS

Introduction	2
What you need to know about the National Tests	3
Preparing and practising for the National Tests	5
The Reading tasks and tests, Levels 1-3: A parent's overview	7
Level 2, Section A: Reading task	
General introductory session	10
Assessment sheet for the general introductory session	11
The Reading running record: Instructions	12
Reading running record	13
Score chart for the Reading running record	14
Discussion of text	15
Assessment of text discussion	17
Assessing the overall grade for Level 2, Section A: Reading task	18
Level 2, Section B: Reading Comprehension test	
A parent's guide	19
Reading Comprehension test	20
Marking the Reading Comprehension test	35
Assessing the overall grade for Section B: Reading Comprehension test	36
Level 3 Reading Comprehension test	
A parent's guide	37
Reading Comprehension test	39
Marking the Reading Comprehension test	47
Assessing the overall grade for the Level 3 Reading Comprehension test	48
Tips to improve your child's reading	48
Level 3 Reader: Food, Glorious Food	1 (49)

INTRODUCTION

YOUR CHILD AND KEY STAGE 1 NATIONAL TESTS

All pupils in Year 2 (ages 6 to 7) will take National Tests or Tasks (practical activities) in English and Mathematics. These important tests and tasks are designed to be an objective assessment of the work your child will have done during Key Stage 1 of the National Curriculum.

Pupils will also have their school work assessed by their teachers. The assessments will be set alongside your child's results in the National Tests to give a clear picture of his or her overall achievement.

In July, the results of your child's tests, together with the teacher assessments, will be reported to you.

HOW THIS BOOK WILL HELP YOUR CHILD

There is plenty of practice in the types of questions he or she will face in the Key Stage 1 National Tests for English: Reading.

The author provides answers and a marking scheme to allow you to check how your child has done.

Using the information in 'Tips to improve your child's reading' (page 48) you can give your child assistance to improve his or her reading skills.

There is a marking grid to record your child's results and to help you estimate the level of the National Curriculum at which your child is working.

The tasks will be carried out between January and June 1998 and the tests will be performed in May 1998.

WHAT YOU NEED TO KNOW ABOUT THE NATIONAL TESTS

KEY STAGE 1 TESTS – HOW THEY WORK

Between the ages of five and seven (Years 1–2), children cover Key Stage 1 of the National Curriculum. From January to June of Year 2, in the final year of Key Stage 1, they are given tasks and tests (commonly known as SATs) in English and Mathematics. The tasks and tests are carried out under the supervision of teachers in school. They are also marked by teachers. The results are then brought together for comparison by external moderators.

Progress in Science, on the other hand, is based on children's performance throughout Key Stage 1 according to teacher assessment.

The tasks and tests in the core subjects, English and Mathematics, help to find out what the children have learned. They also help parents and teachers to know whether the children are reaching the national standards set out in the National Curriculum.

The tasks and tests will provide a brief summary in Year 2 of your child's attainment at that point, whilst teacher assessment is based on the full range of his or her work in relation to the Programmes of Study (the detail of what pupils should be taught for each Key Stage).

When the school has the final collated results of the children's tasks and tests, the results are reported to you as parents by the end of July in the same year. Together with those results, you will receive the results of classroom assessments made by the teachers, based on the work your child has done during the school year. In addition, you will be given a summary of the results for the other children in the school, and for children nationally. This will help you to know how well your child is doing compared with other children of the same age.

The school's report will explain to you what the results show about your child's progress, strengths, particular achievements and targets for development. It will also explain how to follow up the results with the teachers and why the task/test results may differ from their assessment.

WHY THE KEY STAGE 1 TASKS AND TESTS ARE IMPORTANT

Naturally, it is important that children do as well as they can in their national tasks and tests. For although the results are not used to determine what class your child will move up into, in Key Stage 2, they inevitably provide the next teacher with a picture of his or her child's overall attainment.

LEVELS OF ACHIEVEMENT: KNOWING HOW WELL YOUR CHILD IS DOING

The National Curriculum divides each subject into a number of levels, from 1 to 8. On average, children are expected to advance one level for every two years they are at school. It is reasonable to expect that by the end of Key Stage 1, most children should be between Levels 1 and 3, Level 2 being the level which the majority is expected to reach. On very rare occasions, a child at the end of Key Stage 1 may achieve Level 4. This should be recognised as an exceptional result. The following table includes the levels for 7 to 11 year-olds (for the end of Key Stages 1 and 2) to give you an overall picture of how your child should progress.

WHAT YOU NEED TO KNOW ABOUT THE NATIONAL TESTS

			7 years	11 years
■	Exceptional performance	Level 6		■
		Level 5		■
■	Exceeded targets for age group	Level 4	■	■
		Level 3	■	■
■	Achieved targets for age group	Level 2	■	■
■	Working towards targets for age group	Level 1	■	■

YOUR CHILD COMPARED WITH HIS OR HER AGE GROUP

There are different Key Stage 1 national tasks and tests for different attainment levels. This is to ensure that pupils can undertake a task or test where they can show positive achievement, and that they are not discouraged by trying to answer questions which are too easy or too difficult.

This book concentrates on Levels 2 and 3, giving plenty of practice to achieve the best level possible. Children who are able to achieve Level 3 are already above that achieved by the majority in their age group. The table below shows you what percentage of pupils, nationally, reached each of the levels in the 1997 tests for English.

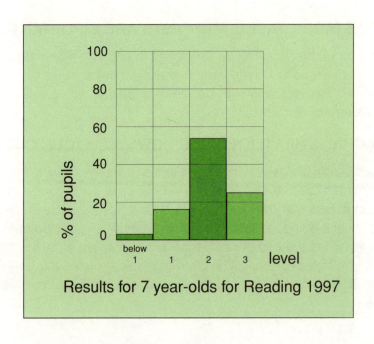

Results for 7 year-olds for Reading 1997

PREPARING AND PRACTISING FOR THE NATIONAL TESTS

ENGLISH AT KEY STAGE 1

The questions in this book will help you prepare your child by testing him or her on the Key Stage 1 curriculum for English: Reading. For assessment purposes, the current National Curriculum divides English into three sections, called Attainment Targets. The first AT, Speaking and Listening, is assessed only by the teacher in the classroom, not in written tests. The other two ATs are :

AT2 Reading

AT3 Writing

The National Curriculum for English defines the level description for each of the three ATs, and the test papers have questions covering AT2 and AT3. Spelling is tested through the child's independent writing and through a spelling test. Handwriting is assessed through the writing task or by copying several sentences from the child's independent writing.

USING THIS BOOK TO HELP YOUR CHILD PREPARE FOR THE NATIONAL TESTS IN ENGLISH: READING

The book contains four basic features:

1 Questions: tasks (Level 2) and tests (Levels 2 and 3) in Reading.

2 Answers: showing acceptable responses and marks.

3 Level charts: showing you how to translate your child's score into a National Curriculum level.

4 Guidance for parents: tips and suggestions to help your child improve his or her reading skills.

Details of how to run the tasks and tests are given on the next page. Information about how to mark the tests and assess your child can be found at the end of each section.

In the margin of each question page for the Levels 2 and 3 Reading Comprehension tests there are small boxes, divided in half, with the marks available for that question at the bottom and a blank at the top for you to fill in with your child's score.

PREPARING AND PRACTISING FOR THE NATIONAL TESTS

SIMULATING TEST CONDITIONS

Allow as much time as your child requires for both the Level 2 tasks and the Levels 2 and 3 tests (this is what will happen in school). The tasks and tests should be carried out somewhere your child feels comfortable, and on different occasions.

Note that your child should only attempt Level 3 activities if he or she has already completed Level 2 successfully.

Detailed requirements of the way to approach each test can be found at the beginning of each section.

MARKING THE QUESTIONS

Guidance on how to mark your child's answers to the questions is given with each section. See the Contents page.

FINALLY, AS THE TASKS AND TESTS DRAW NEAR

As the time for the National Tests approaches, make sure your child is as relaxed and confident as possible. You can help by encouraging your child to believe in him or herself and the teacher! Remind your child of the need to concentrate, but to minimise tension encourage him or her to enjoy these tests. Remember, at this stage most children won't be aware that they are taking formal tests.

Look out for signs of anxiety. Although many children look forward to tests, it is only natural that some may be nervous if they are aware that the tests will take place. Reassure your child that, though important, the tasks and tests are not the only means by which pupils will be assessed.

THE READING TASKS AND TESTS, LEVELS 1–3

A PARENT'S OVERVIEW

Reading at Key Stage 1 is assessed in a number of ways. Children are expected to talk about print, to read extracts from books, to respond verbally to what they have read, and to answer specific questions in written form. The format of the assessment is modelled around specific tasks and tests appropriate to individual levels.

Below you will find a brief description of each task and test, carefully designed to match the expectations of children working at Levels 2 and 3. For parents of children working at Level 1, there is guidance as to how you can best help your child to achieve his or her full potential.

Level 1

Although this book does not aim to provide a specific task to assess Level 1 Reading, it may be of use to you to understand the areas of Reading which are being concentrated on at this level.

Here are some sample activities and questions you could try with your child.

- Go to the local library and ask your child to choose a book to read.
- Ask why he or she chose the book. You may prompt by asking questions such as: 'Do you like the front cover?' or 'Have you read any other books like this one?'
- Look for evidence of your child finding meaning in print. For example, ask questions such as: 'Are there any words in the title that you recognise?' or 'What sound does this word start with?' or 'How many words are there in the title?'

The aim of this is to ensure that your child understands that it is primarily through print that meaning is created. Do not, however, discourage your child from looking for clues about the print through the pictures. For example, if he or she is struggling to read and understand a certain word, and looks at the pictures to seek a clue, this is fine! It is an important stage that all children go through when learning to read.

In school, children who do not achieve Level 1 in this Reading task will be awarded Level 'W', which stands for 'Working towards Level 1'. Attaining 'W' shows some achievement which the Level 1 task will record.

THE READING TASKS AND TESTS, LEVELS 1-3

Level 2

The Level 2 Reading tasks and tests are divided into two main sections as follows:

Section A) task

1. A general introductory session to discuss a specific book. (In this case the book is entitled *The Tough Princess*.)

2. You and your child read part way through the book, and then your child continues to read it on his or her own. (You may only provide help when your child is irretrievably stuck, and this help is then deducted from the overall score.) While your child reads, you make notes on a Reading running record sheet.

3. Your child then responds to what he or she has read, possibly by answering specific questions posed by you.

Section B) test

A paper and pencil Reading Comprehension test based on two passages, one being fiction, the other non-fiction.

Level 3

The Level 3 Reading test is entirely in the form of a paper and pencil test which is administered by an adult, but which your child completes independently. It has three parts to it as follows:

1. A story about which your child answers questions on a test paper.

2. A set of instructions for making something: your child answers questions on the instructions.

3. Three contrasting information passages, which encourage your child to compare differing texts.

How can I tell which level my child should start at?

In school, your child's teacher will assess the level at which your child should start, by using a range of criteria. However, to enable this process to take place in the home, it would be most sensible to begin at Level 1 and work your way up with your child. The charts provided for assessing the Level 2 tasks and tests give clear guidance as to whether your child should go on to attempt the Level 3 Reading test.

Assessment

A form of assessment is provided at the end of each activity. This is intended to reflect as closely as possible how your child's tasks and tests will be assessed in school. However, the Level 2 Reading task is an exception. In school, this task is not marked formally in the way suggested here, but the teacher takes into account all aspects of the Level 2 Reading task to arrive at an overall score. To enable this process to take place in the home, the task has been divided into three specific sections, each one resulting in a score. The three scores are then amalgamated to come up with one overall score for the Level 2 Reading task (see page 18).

THE READING TASKS AND TESTS, LEVELS 1–3

How are the texts chosen for the Reading tasks and tests?

When children carry out tasks and tests in Year 2 of their schooling, the texts which they will have to read and respond to are chosen very carefully, using strict criteria to reflect the abilities and understanding of children at this age.

The test writers choose the texts according to the criteria set out below and to a number of 'readability' criteria.

For the Level 2 Reading task, the teacher chooses three or four texts with which the child is unfamiliar, and which reflect his or her needs and interests. The child then chooses independently which book to read from the selection offered by the teacher.

The list below shows you the criteria for choosing books, to enable you to select other books to share and discuss with your child:

- interesting subject matter to which your child will be able to relate
- interesting characters, who engage the interest of your child
- a clear storyline
- language common to children's literature, such as fairy tale language
- language which displays repetition within the text enabling the reader to become familiar with the style of vocabulary
- language which benefits from reading aloud
- a story with a clear message or purpose
- engaging illustrations.

LEVEL 2
SECTION A: READING TASK

GENERAL INTRODUCTORY SESSION

What to do

Before attempting these tasks, it is a good idea to discuss some of the ideas set down on page 48: 'Tips to improve your child's reading' with your child.

The assessment sheet on which to record your observations is to be found on the next page.

Begin by asking your child what he or she can find out about the book from the front and back covers. You should ask your child the following questions.

- Who wrote this book?
- Have you read any other books by this author?
- What do you think it's going to be about?
  (Children can usually find this information on the back cover of their book.)
- What kind of pictures are in this book?
- Who is the illustrator?
- Which company published the book?
- Where can you find the bar code?
- What's the bar code for?
  (It's so that the bookshop can identify the book and price electronically.)

LEVEL 2
SECTION A: READING TASK

ASSESSMENT SHEET FOR THE GENERAL INTRODUCTORY SESSION

Please place a tick below where you think an achievement description describes the response of your child.

GENERAL INTRODUCTORY SESSION

- child is aware of author ☐
- child knows other books by this author ☐
- child can predict what story may be about ☐
- child can comment on illustrations ☐
- child can locate publisher's logo/name ☐
- child can locate the bar code ☐
- child is aware of purpose of bar code ☐

HOW TO ASSESS LEVEL/GRADE ACHIEVED

Count the number of ticks in the above chart, then transfer them to a level and grade, as shown below.

Score achieved by child	Level/grade
1 – 2	2C
3 – 4	2B
5 – 7	2A

Score _____   Level/grade _____

LEVEL 2
SECTION A: READING TASK

THE READING RUNNING RECORD

INSTRUCTIONS

The purpose of this record is to assess the fluency of your child's reading.

In school, your child's teacher will not add up the number of words read correctly to arrive at a level, but will instead use a range of criteria, thereby employing his or her professional judgement. To enable this assessment to take place in the home, the process has been modified to make it less formal.

WHAT TO DO

- Read the beginning of the book (*The Tough Princess*) with your child, until you arrive at the set passage for the Reading running record (see page 13).
- Ask your child to continue reading the story on his or her own in a clear and slow voice, until reaching the end of the set passage.
- You must tick the boxes on the Reading running record sheet to denote that your child has read the words correctly.
- If your child mis-reads a word, but the sentence still makes sense, simply write the character 's' in the appropriate box to denote 'sense'.
- If your child is absolutely unable to read a word or to make a sensible guess, provide the word for your child, but write the character 'x' in the box to denote a complete omission.
- If the attempt your child makes at an unknown word is plainly incorrect, similarly mark that box with the character 'x'.

ADDITIONAL GUIDANCE

It is extremely important that you take time over the reading of the first part of the book, to give your child a chance to become familiar with the kind of vocabulary in the text. Many of the words are common to fairy tales, and are repeated regularly throughout the book. Remember to look at, and talk about, the pictures – they help the child to make sense of the story.

Do not rush your child during the reading of the set passage. It is important that your child should have ample time when making an attempt at unfamiliar words. Only give the word when your child is clearly stuck.

When your child has finished reading the set passage, read to the end of the book with him or her.

LEVEL 2
SECTION A: READING TASK

READING RUNNING RECORD SHEET

The	King	went	off	into	the	deep	dark
wood	to	annoy	some	bad	fairies.	The	first
fairy	the	King	met	was	no	use.	She
was	a	good	one.	She	didn't	even	get
angry	when	the	King	called	her	names.	The
second	fairy	was	bad,	but	she	was	only
a	beginner.	She	turned	the	King	into	a
frog	for	making	faces	at	her	cat,	but
the	spell	wore	off.	The	third	fairy	was
very	bad.	This	is	her.	The	King	was
awfully	rude	to	her.	'Aha!'	cried	the	Bad
Fairy.	'What	do	you	love	most	in	the
world?'	'My	daughter, Rosamund!'					

Score		Level/grade	

LEVEL 2
SECTION A: READING TASK

SCORE CHART FOR THE READING RUNNING RECORD

The passage that was chosen for the Reading running record contained 100 words. Count up how many words your child read correctly (this includes words marked with the character 's' up to a maximum of 10, but not words marked with the character 'x').

Write the score at the bottom of the Reading running record sheet on page 13.

There are three levels of accuracy in Reading awarded at Level 2: 2A, 2B and 2C (A being the highest and C being the lowest). Look at the chart below to determine the level/grade of your child's reading.

Number of words marked correct	Level/grade
60–75	2C
76–90	2B
91–100	2A

If your child scores between 0 and 59, it means that Level 2 has not been achieved. If this is the case then help your child with lots of reading and by talking to him or her about the books being read. Try the task again at a later stage.

LEVEL 2
SECTION A: READING TASK

DISCUSSION OF TEXT

The next stage of the Reading task is to assess your child's individual response to the story. You are aiming to assess his or her understanding of the story, and ability to interpret what has been read.

When your child takes this test at school, the focus will be more teacher-orientated, in that the teacher will lead the discussion referring to a set of criteria. The questions will not be as specific as here, and the answers will not be marked in the same way. They are provided in this way here to simplify the process for you.

Below is a list of questions placed under different category headings. Ask your child these questions (you may re-word them if you feel it is appropriate), and tick the box which coincides most closely with his or her response. If you feel that your child is struggling to come up with an answer, read aloud the options printed after each question and ask him or her to pick the most appropriate response.

Questions about the characters

1. What is the name of the Princess?

   | Rosalind ☐ | Rosamund ☐ | Rosemary ☐ | Ruby ☐ |

2. How would you describe the King and Queen?

   | happy ☐ | sad ☐ | funny ☐ | unlucky ☐ |

3. How would you describe the Princess?

   | gentle ☐ | polite ☐ | adventurous ☐ | nervous ☐ |

4. Was the third Bad Fairy successful at casting spells?

   Yes ☐   No ☐

Questions about the story

1. Why did the King want the Queen to have a baby boy?

   | Because boys are tougher. ☐ | Because he preferred boys' names. ☐ |
   | Because a boy would make them rich again. ☐ | Because he didn't like girls. ☐ |

LEVEL 2
SECTION A: READING TASK

2   Why wouldn't the Princess allow her father to choose a husband for her?

| Because she wanted to find one for herself. ☐ | Because she didn't like him. ☐ |
| Because he had bad taste. ☐ | Because she didn't want a husband. ☐ |

3   What did the Princess find in the Enchanted Castle?

| treasure ☐ | a handsome prince ☐ |
| a witch ☐ | a fairy ☐ |

4   Why did the Prince and Princess fall in love?

| Because they were both rich. ☐ | Because he thought she was pretty. ☐ |
| Because they liked fighting. ☐ | Because a spell had been cast on them. ☐ |

Questions about the book as a whole

1   Why is this story unusual for a fairy tale?

| Because princes and princesses are normally gentle to each other. ☐ | Because fairy tales normally have bears in them. ☐ |

2   What is the usual role of a witch in fairy tales?

| To be helpful and kind. ☐ | To tell the story. ☐ |
| To make you laugh. ☐ | To cast successful spells on others. ☐ |

LEVEL 2
SECTION A: READING TASK

ASSESSMENT OF TEXT DISCUSSION

Fill in the chart below with the scores achieved by your child in each of the sections.

Questions about the characters:	/4
Questions about the story:	/4
Questions about the book as a whole:	/2
Total:	/10

Now transfer your child's score to a level, using the conversion chart below.

Number of correct answers	Level/grade
4–6	2C
7–8	2B
9–10	2A

If your child scores between 1 and 3, it means that Level 2 has not been achieved.

Level/grade

LEVEL 2
SECTION A: READING TASK

ASSESSING THE OVERALL GRADE FOR LEVEL 2 SECTION A: READING TASK

Your child will now have three levels and grades for the Level 2 Reading task. These include a level and grade for the general introductory session, a level and grade for the Reading running record, and a level and grade for discussion of the text.

Follow these guidelines to assess your child's overall grade for the Level 2 Reading task:

Scores achieved by child	Overall score
2A 2A 2A	2A
2A 2A 2B	2A
2A 2B 2B	2B
2B 2B 2B	2B
2B 2B 2C	2B
2B 2C 2C	2C
2C 2C 2C	2C

It does not matter in what order the scores are achieved for the individual sections. For example, 2C 2B 2C is still awarded an overall score of 2C.

Overall level/grade achieved for Section A: Reading task

Continue on to Level 2, Section B: Reading Comprehension test after a suitable break – perhaps return to it on another day.

Note to parents

See page 48 for an important and useful guide to helping your child improve his or her reading: *Tips to improve your child's reading*.

LEVEL 2
SECTION B: READING COMPREHENSION TEST

A PARENT'S GUIDE

Explain to your child that there are two sections to this test: the first takes the form of a story, and the second is an information passage. Both texts are interspersed with questions which your child should answer in written form while working through the test.

Explain that there is no time limit in which the answers should be completed. If you feel that your child would achieve a better result by completing the test one section at a time, that is fine.

At the beginning of each of the sections you will find two practice questions. It is important that you use these questions to familiarise your child with the format of the test. Your child will either be required to tick a box corresponding to the correct answer, or to write an answer in his or her own words on a line underneath the question.

Once you have worked through the practice questions together, your child should continue with the test on his or her own, without being offered further help.

READING
LEVEL 2

MARKS

QUESTIONS LEVEL 2

Frogs' holiday

There is a quiet, peaceful pond near here. But for the frogs who live in the pond it is neither quiet nor peaceful. There are too many big fish and too many small boys.

"We need to get away from this pond. We want a holiday," said the frogs one morning. So, taking some fly-and-spider sandwiches and flasks of pond-water, they hopped up the hill and along the street in search of the perfect place for a frogs' holiday.

Practice question

1 What spoils the pond for the frogs?

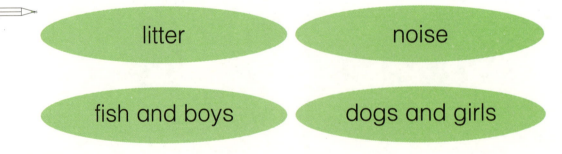

Practice question

2 What do the frogs want?

  ....

20

QUESTIONS LEVEL 2

They looked in the pet shop, but that had too many big fish.

They looked in the swimming-pool, but that had too many small boys.

Then they came to a place that was warm and damp. There were no big fish and no small boys.

It was Mrs Crumple's launderette.
The frogs had found the perfect place for their perfect holiday.

3 What were there too many of in the pet shop?

cats   birds   dogs   fish

4 What was the temperature like in the launderette?

....

They waited until the last customer went home, and Mrs Crumple locked up the shop and went upstairs. Then... they had lots and lots of fun.

Mrs Crumple came back downstairs with a large bag of her own washing.

"What's going on?" cried Mrs Crumple.

5   When the frogs began their fun, where had Mrs Crumple gone?

- to the shops
- upstairs
- to the back door
- on holiday

6   Why did Mrs Crumple come downstairs again?

QUESTIONS LEVEL 2

"Out by morning!" ordered Mrs Crumple.

"But we want a holiday," wailed all the frogs.

"I need a holiday," said Mrs Crumple.

"Then off you go," said the frogs, "and we'll mind the shop and the baby as well."

So the next day, the frogs washed towels for the hairdresser, folded sheets, and made sure that people behaved properly in Mrs Crumple's launderette.

They also kept the baby fed... and cheerful... and clean.

At the end of the day they were tired but happy.

7 Who did the frogs wash towels for?

8 How did the frogs feel at the end of the day?

happy   sad   angry   bored

READING LEVEL 2

MARKS

QUESTIONS LEVEL 2

Mrs Crumple went to the quiet, peaceful pond with her fishing gear.

She had a nice long sit-down, and a cup of tea and some jam sandwiches.

Then, feeling much refreshed, she caught a big fish and chased lots of small boys.

At the end of the day she was tired but happy. She thanked the frogs for her day off.

9 Where did Mrs Crumple spend her day off?

- the park
- the zoo
- the seaside
- the pond

1 Q9

10 What did Mrs Crumple have in her picnic? Name two things.

....

....

1 Q10

24

QUESTIONS LEVEL 2

She went into her little back room and made the frogs some fishpaste sandwiches and opened a packet of squashed-fly biscuits.

Next morning the frogs said goodbye to Mrs Crumple and thanked her for their wonderfully quiet holiday.

11 What sandwiches did Mrs Crumple make for the frogs?

- fishpaste
- cheese
- squashed-fly
- egg

12 How did the frogs describe their holiday?

....

They went back along the street, and down the hill to the pond, where life is always too exciting.

And whenever the frogs want a holiday, they go back to Mrs Crumple's launderette and give her a day off. It is the most perfect place for a frogs' holiday.

13 What word would the frogs use to describe their usual life?

   dull   sleepy   exciting   busy

14 Where is the frogs' most perfect holiday place?

QUESTIONS LEVEL 2

READING LEVEL 2

MARKS

The frogs sent this thank-you letter to Mrs Crumple.

> The Busy Pond
> Frog Town
> 1st July
>
> Dear Mrs Crumple,
> We would like to invite you to come and stay with us on 5th July. We will be waiting for you in the pond at 4 o'clock in the afternoon. The weather forecast is good, so you will be able to go fishing! We will have a picnic of worm burgers and pickled spiders.
> See you then!
> With love from
> The frogs.

15 What date have the frogs invited Mrs Crumple to the pond?

....

1 Q15

16 What time do they expect her to arrive?

....

1 Q16

17 What will Mrs Crumple be able to do when she gets there?

....

1 Q17

18 What food will they eat? Name two things.

....

1 Q18

27

Letts

READING
LEVEL 2

MARKS

QUESTIONS
LEVEL 2

Holidays

Introduction

Have you ever been on holiday?

Lots of people look forward to their holidays because it means that they can relax and have some fun!

Some people go abroad to other countries for their holidays. Others stay closer to home.

London is one of the most popular holiday places in the world. Read on and find out more about England's capital city.

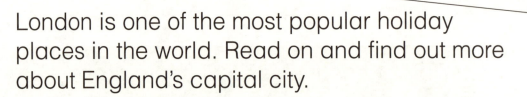

1   On holiday people may like to

   relax and have fun   read

   swim   sun-bathe

2   What is the name of the capital city of England?

....

28

QUESTIONS LEVEL 2

The history of London

People have lived in London for many thousands of years, even as far back as prehistoric times. We know this because tools and weapons made of flint have been found in the area. They belonged to prehistoric people.

All sorts of settlers chose London as a great trading place, thanks to its position next to the River Thames.

There are many places and landmarks in London today, which date back many hundreds of years. The Tower of London was built in the year 1078; the British Museum opened in 1759; and the Houses of Parliament were rebuilt after a fire in 1834, during the reign of Queen Victoria.

3 How do we know that people were living in London in prehistoric times?

4 Why was London a good trading place?

5 What building was opened in 1759?

....

6 Why were the Houses of Parliament rebuilt?

- They were falling down.
- They were old fashioned.
- They burnt down.
- They were unsafe.

QUESTIONS LEVEL 2

READING LEVEL 2

MARKS

Famous London landmarks

Westminster Abbey is one of the most famous landmarks in London, and also one of the oldest. It is one of the most important churches in the country. Many kings and queens have been crowned, married and buried there.

Near the entrance to the Abbey is the tomb of the Unknown Soldier. Here, people can remember all the soldiers who died in the two world wars.

The Houses of Parliament are situated across the road from Westminster Abbey. It is here that decisions on how to run the country are made. The people who make the laws are called politicians.

In November 1605, Guy Fawkes tried to blow up the Houses of Parliament, but he was caught just in time. Since then, every year, people celebrate his capture by burning models of him on a bonfire and by letting off fireworks.

Buckingham Palace is the London home of the Queen, and stands at the end of a long road called The Mall. When the Queen is at home, a flag is flown above the balcony at the front of the Palace.

READING LEVEL 2

QUESTIONS LEVEL 2

MARKS

7 What kinds of important people have been married in Westminster Abbey?

- actors
- politicians
- footballers
- kings and queens

1 Q7

8 Where are the Houses of Parliament?

1 Q8

9 Who tried to blow them up?

1 Q9

10 How can you tell if the Queen is at home?

1 Q10

Transport

There are many different ways of getting around London, but the most common ways are by bus and underground. London buses are red with two levels; they are known as 'double deckers'.  The underground is a network of trains which run along narrow tunnels under the ground all around London. The first underground train line was opened in 1862 and ran between Baker Street and the City.

It is also possible to get around London by car, taxi or boat.

11 What colour are London buses?

red   blue   green   yellow

12 Why are London buses called 'double deckers'?

....

READING LEVEL 2

MARKS

Q13

Q14

QUESTIONS LEVEL 2

13 In which year was the first underground train line opened?

(1962) (1682) (1862) (1692)

14 Name another way you can get around London, apart from by bus or underground.

✎ ....

| Score | | Grade/level | |

MARKING THE LEVEL 2 READING COMPREHENSION TEST

Note to parents

Before you mark your child's answers, please re-read the two passages to ensure that you are entirely familiar with their content. This will help you to follow the marking key in a clear way, and to assess the appropriateness of your child's answers. Different children have different ways of wording the correct answer. Concentrate on the content of their response, assessing whether your child 'had the right idea'.

The multiple-choice questions are more easily marked; they are either right or wrong. However, if your child ticks more than one answer, no marks may be awarded. If, by mistake, your child does not answer a question in the manner asked for (for example, if he or she crosses a box instead of ticking it), you should still allow the point if it has been answered correctly.

As you mark the test, insert the score for each question in the box provided at the edge of each page, always referring back to the marking key to ensure you are apportioning the correct number of marks to each question.

Finally, your child should not be penalised for poor handwriting or spelling; these are not the focuses of this test. Nor does your child need to write in complete sentences.

Frogs' holiday

1	Fish and boys.	*Practice*
2	A holiday.	*Practice*
3	Fish.	1
4	Warm/hot.	1
5	Upstairs.	1
6	To do her washing.	1
7	The hairdresser.	1
8	Happy.	1
9	The pond.	1
10	Tea, jam sandwiches.	1
	Both answers must be provided to score the point.	
11	Fishpaste.	1
12	Wonderfully quiet/quiet.	1
13	Exciting.	1
14	Mrs Crumple's launderette/a launderette.	1
15	5th July.	1
16	4 o'clock (in the afternoon).	1
17	Go fishing.	1
18	Worm burgers, pickled spiders.	1
	Both answers must be provided to score the point.	

MARKING THE LEVEL 2 READING COMPREHENSION TEST

Holidays

1	Relax and have fun.	*Practice*
2	London.	*Practice*
3	Tools and weapons have been found in the area.	1
4	Because it is next to the River Thames.	1
5	The British Museum.	1
6	They burnt down.	1
7	Kings and queens.	1
8	Opposite/across the road from Westminster Abbey.	1
9	Guy Fawkes.	1
10	The flag will fly (at Buckingham Palace).	1
11	Red.	1
12	Because they have two levels.	1
13	1862.	1
14	Car/taxi/boat.	1

Any or all of these answers may be accepted.

The maximum score is 28.

Assessing the overall grade for Level 2, Section B: Reading Comprehension test

When your child has completed the test, add up the number of marks awarded and fill in the total in the box provided at the end of the Reading test on page 34. Then use the table below to assess the level achieved.

Number of marks (inclusive)	0-9	10-20	21-24	25-28
Level	Level 2 not achieved	Level 2C achieved	Level 2B achieved	Level 2A achieved

What to do with these results

Your child will now have two scores for his or her reading at Level 2: one from the task in Section A and the other from the test in Section B. If your child has achieved Level 2A in the Reading task, he or she should continue on to the Level 3 Reading Comprehension test. If your child achieved Level 2B in the task, but Level 2A in the Reading Comprehension test, it is still worthwhile to allow your child to attempt the Level 3 Reading Comprehension test. If your child scored below this level he or she should not attempt the Level 3 test.

Always allow a break between tests! Also always remember to praise your child for what he or she has achieved, whatever the outcome.

LEVEL 3
READING COMPREHENSION TEST

A PARENT'S GUIDE

To answer the questions for the Level 3 Reading Comprehension test, your child needs to read carefully the reader situated at the back of this book (pages 1–12) entitled *Food, Glorious Food*. Tear it out carefully along the perforations, and clip or staple it together. Before your child begins, you need to make sure that you are thoroughly familiar with it yourself.

Look at the reader together with your child. Make sure that your child is aware that there are three separate sections to it: a story; a set of instructions; and an information passage. There is also an introductory section.

Explain that there is no time limit in which the answers should be completed. If you feel that your child would achieve a better result by completing the test one section at a time, this is fine. Explain to your child that it is necessary to read a whole section through thoroughly first, before attempting to answer the corresponding questions.

Your child needs to work through each section on his or her own. Once you have gone through the initial practice questions, you should not offer further help.

Your child needs the reader and the Reading Comprehension test section (pages 39-46) as he or she works through the test.

Now turn to the practice questions on page 39, and help your child to answer them correctly.

Ask your child to look at the practice questions. Explain that there are two practice questions that you would like them to write down the answer to. Read the first question with your child. Ask them to tick the box which displays the correct answer to the question.

Check that your child has understood what needs to be done.

Now ask your child to read the second question, and to write the answer on the lines underneath. If they make a mistake, let them know that it is perfectly all right to erase or cross out an answer. They will not lose any marks.

Allow your child enough time to answer each question.

Check the answers your child has given. If you feel confident that they have understood the task, allow them to continue with the rest of the Reading test.

Finally, read through the final instructions on page 38 to your child (you may adapt them if you feel it makes it easier for your child), and then your child may begin.

Ask your child to turn to the Introduction on page 1 of the reader.

Carefully read the Introduction on pages 1 and 2 to your child. Ask him or her to follow the words as you read.

LEVEL 3
READING COMPREHENSION TEST

FINAL INSTRUCTIONS

- Your child may look at the reader as often as he or she wishes whilst answering the questions.

- Your child will be asked to answer questions in a number of ways, such as putting a tick in a box, circling a correct answer, writing a sentence, or linking together two parts of an answer.

- Your child will not be penalised for incorrect spelling.

QUESTIONS LEVEL 3

Introduction

1 What do all living things need to keep them alive?

clothes   food   milk   insects

2 What does the piece of writing Cheesy Tomatoes show you how to make?

....

Now please wait until you are told to continue with the rest of the Reading test.

Mrs Wobble the Waitress

3 Why did Mrs Wobble lose her job at the café?

- Because she was rude to the customers.
- Because she could not add up.
- Because she was a mess.
- Because she kept on dropping the food.

4 Why wouldn't Mrs Wobble be able to get a job as a waitress somewhere else?

....

....

5 Put rings around two things the children bought to use in their new café.

- roller-skates
- aprons
- shoes
- tape measures
- paint
- a fishing net

QUESTIONS LEVEL 3

6 What does Mr Wobble mean when he says, "We are going to make our fortunes"?

....

7 Finish the matching to show what jobs each of the Wobble family did to prepare for the new café.

Master Wobble	laid the tables.
Mrs Wobble and Miss Wobble	began cooking.
Mr Wobble	went round the town with a sandwich board.

8 Put a ring around the word which describes how the customers felt as they saw the children chasing and catching the food.

happy   sad   silly   annoyed

READING LEVEL 3

MARKS

Q9

QUESTIONS LEVEL 3

9 Look at the last sentence of the story. Why is Mrs Wobble worried that she might **not** wobble?

 ....

....

Q10

10 Here are some events in the story. Put them in the correct order by numbering each box. The first one has been done for you.

Mrs Wobble loses her job.	The children catch the food in their nets.	They turn their house into a café.	The family make their fortune.
1			

42

QUESTIONS LEVEL 3

Cheesy Tomatoes

11 What is the teaspoon used for?

- To eat the tomatoes with.
- To serve the tomatoes.
- To scoop out the flesh.
- To cut the tomatoes.

12 Put a ring around the ingredient which is mixed up with the tomato flesh in the bowl.

cheese   salt   butter   parsley

13 In which 2 ways can you tell when the tomatoes have been cooked properly?

....

....

14 How do you think the tomatoes that Michael made would have tasted ?

....

15 This is the Contents page of a cookery book:

Contents			
Cooking and safety	10	**Salad recipes**	24
		Cucumber salad	25
Egg and cheese recipes	12	Surprise tomatoes	26
Soft boiled egg	13	Potato salad	28
Fried egg sandwich	15		
Cheesy tomatoes	17	**Ice cream recipes**	30
		Chocolate delight	32
Sausage recipes	18	Knickerbocker Glory	34
Sausage casserole	20	Banana Rhumba	35
Sausages on sticks	22	Baked Alaska	36

To find out how to make Banana Rhumba, you would turn to page 35.

Which page would you turn to, to find:

a   Another recipe which uses tomatoes?

page ....

b   How to work safely in the kitchen?

page ....

QUESTIONS LEVEL 3

Chips, Chocolate and Milk

Chips

16 Who or what eats the unwanted potato skins after they have been removed?

- the factory workers
- fish
- animals
- plants

17 What are 'nubbins'?

....

....

Chocolate

18 Put a ring around the number of beans you may find in a cocoa pod.

- 17
- 39
- 4
- 120

READING LEVEL 3

MARKS

QUESTIONS LEVEL 3

19 What makes the beans get their chocolate flavour?

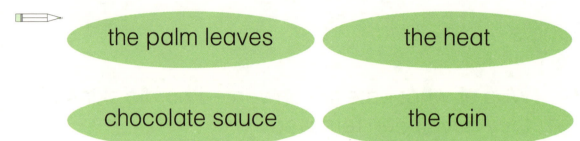

- the palm leaves
- the heat
- chocolate sauce
- the rain

1 mark Q19

Milk

20 What are animals called that make milk for their babies? Put a ring around the correct answer.

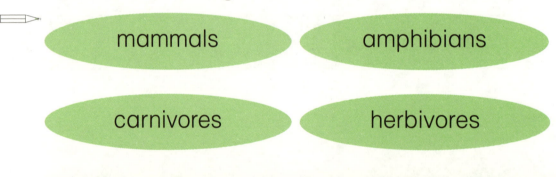

- mammals
- amphibians
- carnivores
- herbivores

1 mark Q20

21 Write down the two most important reasons why you should drink milk.

....

....

2 marks Q21

Score | Level/grade

46

MARKING THE LEVEL 3 READING COMPREHENSION TEST

Note to parents

Before you mark your child's answers, please re-read the reader to ensure that you are entirely familiar with its content. This will help you to follow the marking key in a clear way, and to assess the appropriateness of your child's answers. Different children have different ways of wording a correct answer. Concentrate on the content of their response, assessing whether your child 'had the right idea'.

The multiple-choice questions are more easily marked; they are either right or wrong. However, if your child circles more answers than he or she is asked for, no marks may be awarded. If by mistake your child does not answer a question in the manner asked for, for example if he or she ticks an answer instead of putting a circle around it, you should still allow the point if it has been answered correctly.

As you mark the test, insert the score for each question in the box provided at the edge of each page, always referring back to the marking key to ensure you are apportioning the correct number of marks to each question. Assess the level using the key on page 48.

Finally, your child should not be penalised for poor handwriting or spelling. These are not the focuses of this test. Nor does your child need to write in complete sentences.

Introduction
1 Food. *Practice*
2 A tasty tomato dish. *Practice*

Mrs Wobble the Waitress
3 Because she kept on dropping the food. *1*
4 Because there were no more cafés in the town. *1*
5 Roller-skates, a fishing net. *1*
Both answers must be given to achieve the point.
6 They will become rich. *1*
7 Mrs and Miss Wobble laid the tables. *1*
Mr Wobble began cooking. *Both answers must be given to achieve the point.*
8 Happy. *1*
9 The customers like to see her wobble; it has attracted customers. *1*
10 1 Mrs Wobble loses her job. *1*
   2 They turn their house into a café.
   3 The children catch the food in their nets.
   4 The family make their fortune. *All four answers must be ordered correctly to achieve the point.*

Cheesy Tomatoes
11 To scoop out the flesh. *1*
12 Cheese. *1*
13 The cheese mixture melts. *1*
The cheese mixture browns (lightly). *1*
14 Sweet/sugary. *1*
15 a) 26 *1*
   b) 10 *1*

Chips, Chocolate and Milk
16 Animals. *1*
17 Badly cut chips. *1*
18 39 *1*
19 The heat. *1*
20 Mammals. *1*
21 Milk makes your bones strong. *1*
Milk gives you energy. *1*

The maximum score is 22.

TIPS TO IMPROVE YOUR CHILD'S READING

ASSESSING THE OVERALL GRADE FOR LEVEL 3

When your child has completed the test, add up the number of marks awarded and fill in the total in the box provided at the end of the Reading test on page 46. Then use the table below to assess the level achieved.

Number of marks	0–10	11–22
Level	Level 3 not achieved	Level 3 achieved

TIPS TO IMPROVE YOUR CHILD'S READING

There are many ways that you can help your child with his or her reading. Below you will find a variety of practical suggestions, and examples of the kinds of questions pupils can expect to be asked in their assessment tests.

Sharing books with your child
Read stories with your child, even after he or she has become a fluent reader. Take it in turns to read a page each. Read a page to your child, and then ask him or her to read the same page back to you. Talk about the plot. For example, ask your child to tell the story in his or her own words. Questions to ask: Guess what will happen next. What type of book (or story, poetry, play, information) is it? Is there a message to be learnt from the book?

Authors
Questions to ask: Who is your favourite author? What kind of books does this author write? Can you name other books by the same author?

Characters
Questions to ask: What kind of person (or creature) is...? Can you find a word to describe… ? On this page, what shows you that… is… ?
Suggestions to make: Name some of your favourite fictional characters. Draw your favourite character.

Illustrations
Questions to ask: Do the illustrations tell you anything that the words do not? Who illustrated the book? What style has the illustrator used in these pictures? (For example, pencil drawings, water colours, black and white, cartoons). Are there any other books you know with pictures by the same illustrator? Is the writer the same person as the illustrator in this book? (Mention that sometimes writers illustrate their own books.)

How the book is made
Questions to ask: Which company published the book? How much did it cost? When was it printed? What is its ISBN (publishing number)? What is the bar code for? Is there a summary of the story on the back cover?

Different types of writing
Describe some kinds of writing, such as: fiction, information, poetry, drama, newspaper, magazine, comic. Then ask your child, What kind is this book?

Information
Follow the alphabetical order in a book's Index together, to find out information. Ask your child, What is the difference between the Contents list and the Index? Then get him or her to practise scanning a text to obtain information quickly. Ask your child to see how much he or she can remember afterwards. Show how much information we can get from a newpaper, such as: the news, weather reports and what's on television.

LEVEL 3 READER

Food, Glorious Food

Contents

Introduction	2
Mrs Wobble the Waitress	3
Cheesy Tomatoes	9
Chips	11
Chocolate	13
Milk	14

ENGLISH READER

Introduction

In this reader you will find three pieces of writing about food. Food is very important because all living things need it to keep them alive.

Mrs Wobble the Waitress is about a waitress who loses her job because she wobbles with the food.

Cheesy Tomatoes shows you how to make a tasty tomato dish, and you can find out how chocolate, chips and milk are produced!

Mrs Wobble the Waitress

Written by Allan Ahlberg, pictures by Janet Ahlberg.

Mrs Wobble was a waitress.
She liked her work.
The customers liked her.
The only trouble was – she wobbled.

One day Mrs Wobble wobbled with
a bowl of soup.
The soup landed on a customer's dog.
Mrs Wobble got told off.

The next day Mrs Wobble wobbled
with a roast chicken.
The roast chicken landed on a customer's head.
Mrs Wobble got told off again.

The next day Mrs Wobble wobbled with a plate of jelly.
The jelly landed on the *manager's* head.
Mrs Wobble got the sack.

Mrs Wobble went home to her family.
Mr Wobble cooked her tea.
The children tried to cheer her up.
"Cheer up, Ma!" they said.
"You will find another job –
in another café!"

But there were no other cafés.
That was the only one in town.
Mrs Wobble knew this.
"There are no other cafés," she said
and she began to cry.

The children did not like to see their mother cry.
It made them cry.
It made their father cry too.

Then Mr Wobble had an idea.
"I know what we can do," he said.
"We can open a café of our own."

"Where?" said Mrs Wobble.
"Where?" said Miss Wobble.
"Where?" said Master Wobble.
"Here!" said Mr Wobble.

"We can turn the house into a café!"

The next day the Wobble family
turned their house into a café.
They cleaned and painted.
They moved the chairs and tables around.
They changed the curtains.

Mr Wobble went shopping.
He bought some meat and vegetables,
fruit and fish,
cheese and chicken,
flour and a few other things.

The children went shopping too.
They bought two pairs of roller-skates and a fishing net.
"What are those for?" said
Mr Wobble.
"It's a surprise, Pa," the
children said.
"You wait and see!"

In the evening Mrs
Wobble made
waiter's clothes for her
children,
and a cook's hat for
her husband.
Mr Wobble and the
children made the menus.

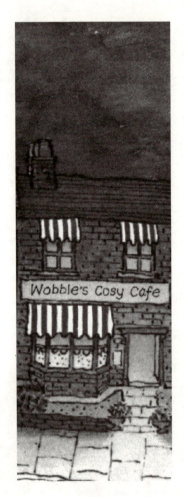

The children went to bed.
Mr and Mrs Wobble stepped outside.
They looked at their new café.
"It's the big day, tomorrow," Mr Wobble said.
"We are going to make our fortunes."
"Yes," said Mrs Wobble.
"The only trouble is – what if I wobble?"

The next day the children woke up early.
"It's the big day, today, Ma," Master Wobble said.
He gave his mother a cup of tea in bed.
Miss Wobble gave her father
a cup of tea in bed.
"We are going to make our fortunes today, Pa," she said.

After breakfast
Mr Wobble began cooking.
Mrs and Miss Wobble laid
the tables.
Master Wobble went
round the town with a
sandwich board.

The first customers
arrived.
"Oh dear," said Mrs
Wobble. "What if I…?"

Mrs Wobble wobbled with a bowl of soup.

"Help!" said the customer.
Miss Wobble skated to the rescue.
She caught the soup in another bowl.
"That's clever," the customer said.

Mrs Wobble wobbled with a roast chicken.
"Wow!" said the customer.

Master Wobble skated to the rescue.
He caught the roast chicken in a net.
"Hooray!" the customer said.

Then all the other customers cheered.
"Hooray, hooray!"
"This is more fun than a circus!" they said.

That night Mrs Wobble counted the money.
"It looks like a fortune to us, Ma," the children said.
Mr Wobble gave them a hug.

"And we owe it all to the
famous juggling waiters!" he said.

The next day there was a big crowd in the street.
The people had come from miles around
to see the famous juggling waiters.

The children peeped out.
"There's a big crowd in the
street, Ma," they said.
"Yes," said Mrs Wobble.
And she began to laugh.
"Now the only trouble is –
what if I *don't* wobble?"

Cheesy Tomatoes

Have a go at making this tasty snack; it's perfect as a supper dish! Ask an adult to help you.

You will need:

Utensils:
sharp knife,
teaspoon,
cheese grater,
mixing bowl,
fork,
spatula,
serving plate.

Ingredients:
  4 tomatoes,
100 grammes grated cheese,
 25 grammes butter,
large pinch of salt.

What to do:

1   Cut the tomatoes in half.
    Ask an adult to help you.

2   Scoop the fleshy centres out, using the teaspoon, and place them in a mixing bowl.

3   Mix together the tomato flesh and the grated cheese using the fork.

4   Spoon the tomato and cheese mixture back into the tomato halves, and dot with butter. Sprinkle salt over the top of the mixture.

5   Place the tomato halves in the grill pan, and grill gently for a few moments until the cheese starts to melt and turn brown. Ask an adult to help you.

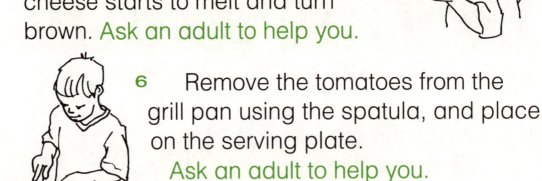

6   Remove the tomatoes from the grill pan using the spatula, and place on the serving plate.
Ask an adult to help you.

Follow the recipe carefully!

When Michael made the cheesy tomatoes, he mistook the sugar for the salt and sprinkled it over the tomatoes! YUK!

Chips

Fish and chips, burger and chips, chicken and chips, pie and chips, egg and chips... What could be better? Chips are one of the most popular foods around these days. So what exactly are chips?

Chips are strips of potato deep-fried in oil. You can make your own chips at home, or you can buy them ready-frozen at the supermarket, or you can buy them ready-cooked from a chip shop. Here's how the factories make them!

First the potatoes are sorted into different sizes and then they are washed. Next, the potato skins are removed and put into large containers, which are sent to farms all over the country. The farmers then feed their animals with a smelly potato skin mixture!

Back in the factory, the potatoes are cut into different sized chips. Any chips not correctly cut are thrown away; these are known as 'nubbins'.

Finally, all the perfect chips are fried very quickly in oil, and frozen and put into bags, ready for us to buy in the supermarket.

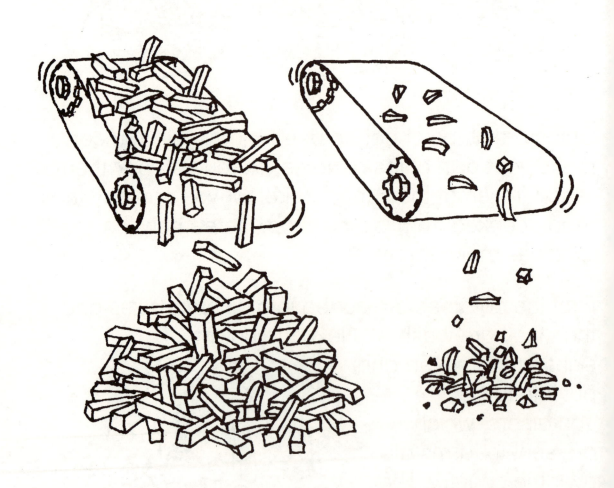

Chocolate

Chocolate is one of the tastiest, sweetest, most delicious luxury foods money can buy! It comes in all sorts of forms: as chocolate bars, on top of a cake, as a drink, or as the topping on a biscuit!

But what is chocolate made of? It grows as cocoa beans in pods on trees. A pod is like a big container, and one pod can hold between twenty and forty cocoa beans. The cocoa beans are treated in a special way to turn them into chocolate.

The beans are taken out of their pods, and buried under a pile of banana leaves; the leaves keep the beans warm, and the heat brings out the lovely cocoa flavour.

Cocoa beans are roasted and turned into chocolate in factories all around the world, so that we can have chocolate eggs at Easter, a mug of drinking choclate at bed-time, and a chocolate bar at any old time.

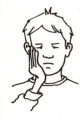

But remember – too much chocolate can be bad for your teeth!

Milk

We use milk for all sorts of reasons: to turn our tea and coffee white, to pour over our breakfast cereal, to make pancakes, or simply to drink as it is. Most of the milk we buy in shops comes from cows, but all sorts of animals produce milk for their babies to drink. These animals, which include human beings, are known as mammals.

Young children, especially, need to drink milk regularly, as it gives them all the goodness they need to make their bones grow strong. It also gives them energy, which young children need lots of!